Hell *Is* Real

Hell *Is* Real

Apostle Wislet Charles

Library of Congress Control Number: 2019919866

PAPERBACK: 978-1-952155-29-1
EBOOK: 978-1-952155-30-7

Scripture quotations marked KJV are from the Holy Bible, King James Version (Authorized Version). First published in 1611. Quoted from the KJV Classic Reference Bible, © 1983 by the Zondervan Corporation.

Ordering Information:

For orders and inquiries, please contact:
1-888-404-1388
www.goldtouchpress.com
book.orders@goldtouchpress.com

Printed in the United States of America

Contents

Hell Is Real (Part 1)

My name is Wislet Charles and I was born on September 7, 1969, in Nassau, New Providence, Bahamas. My parents are Agnes Morrison and Winston Charles. As a child I was the black sheep in my family, and everybody looked down on me because I was a sickly child. As I started to grow up, I felt the hands of God strongly upon my life.

At the age of thirteen years I started to work as a packing boy at Harding's food store at Lyford Cay. I was living on my own. I thought I was my own man and I did my own thing. I was not a Christian. I was not saved. It was at this time that the Lord spoke to me and told me that he wanted to use me for his glory and I refused his voice. Just like the prophet Jeremiah, I began to make excuses and I said, "I am not ready to give my life to God. I am too young. I want to enjoy life first." I said, "Maybe later, but not now." I was stubborn and rebellious.

It was on July 26, 1987, while working at a cement factory at Clifton Pier, Nassau, Bahamas, that my boss asked me one morning to work the cement machine, and it was while working the cement machine that my right hand got stuck in the machine and it started to pull my entire body into the machine. Before I knew it, I was crushed under fifteen hundred pounds of steel, with most of the weight landing on my back. I fainted immediately from the pressure of the weight. Suddenly I heard the voice of God saying ever so gently, "I am not ready for you yet." After that I felt my heart start to beat again, and when my boss saw that I was stuck, he immediately stopped the machine, and I saw that he was afraid. He asked me if I wanted to go to the hospital, but I said, "No, I am fine."

In August 1988 I went to work at Crystal Palace Resort and Casino in Nassau, Bahamas, as a houseman in the housekeeping department. One Wednesday morning I hiked a ride with a Rasta man from Adelaide Village, and he offered to take me directly to work at Crystal Palace Resort. The Rasta, who had probably just finished his morning smoke of marijuana, was driving at least sixty miles per hour, and as he negotiated a dangerous curve on the airport road, the vehicle flipped over in the air at least four times and landed on its tires. Neither the Rasta nor I was injured, and he dropped me off to work. Even after this warning I continued on with my life and did not heed the voice of God.

In that same year (1988) I went to live with my grandaunt Shirley King in an area of Nassau that is known as Rock Crusher. One Friday night, while in the middle of the street with my friends drinking beers and shooting dice, a police car came from behind and hit me at least five feet in the air, and when I hit the ground, I ran as fast as I could because I was afraid that, if I had been caught, I would have been taken to jail.

Three days later my feet started to swell and my aunt Shirley took me to the accident and emergency department of the Princess Margaret Hospital, and when the nurse that was assigned to me took my temperature, it read one hundred and three degrees, which is dangerously high for a human. I was extremely thirsty and I kept asking for water every two or three minutes. At this time I had severe back pains. I also could not urinate, and the doctor that was assigned to me placed a tube through my urethra, which enabled me to pass water. The doctor informed me that I had bladder and kidney problems and that they would have to admit me to the hospital. After three days in the hospital, instead of recovering from my illness, I took a turn for the worse. I could not control my urine or my bowels, and blood was coming from every part of my body. I could not use my hands or feet. I was almost a vegetable. I could not recognize anybody, not even my own mother. After about two weeks, I got well enough to be released from the hospital, but after two days, I again began to cough up and pass blood in my urine. I was admitted to the hospital, and while walking to the male medical ward of Princess Margaret Hospital, I became dizzy and passed out. When I awoke, I found myself hooked up to a life support machine, and tubes were coming out of every part of my body. I was in the hospital for six months and admitted to the intensive care unit (ICU) three times during this period. I had a number of medical problems. I was anemic and I also was plagued with asthma and fainting spells. I was informed by the doctors that were assigned to me that they were running a series of medical tests on me to try to determine why my health was not improving. I was in bad shape. As a matter of fact, my family had already given up on me and said there was no more hope for me, and they started to make preparations for my funeral. But Jeremiah 17:7 says, "Blessed is the man that trusteth in the Lord, and whose hope the Lord is."

It was in December 1988, on my last visit to the hospital while in the ICU, that I died and my spirit left my body. I traveled through this dark tunnel, and suddenly I arrived at this very dark place and I started to sweat profusely because it was extremely hot. I arrived at this gigantic black gate, and the gate swung open on its own accord. As it opened, I heard a loud bang. As the Spirit of the Lord led me through this dark place, I heard many voices screaming and crying, saying, "Help me! Help me!" And as I continued on, I saw many dark spirits and they made very scary sounds, sounds that are indescribable. There were worms and the stench of rotting flesh and fire was everywhere. I knew I was in hell. In Mark 9:44, Jesus says, in hell, "[their] worm[s] dieth not, and the fire is not quenched." I saw as I walked through hell huge caves off to my right side. I also saw many coffins, and in these coffins I saw pastors. How did I know they were pastors? It is because they had their pastor's collars around their necks. I saw demons throw some form of corrosive substance into these coffins and then strike them with their spears, and I also saw fire under every coffin, and the pastors would scream aloud from the pain that was being inflicted upon them by the demons. At this time I started to cry because of the hopeless state of those pastors. As I traveled on I saw many demons. Some of which were half-human and half-animal; their faces, hands, and chests were in human form but their thighs and legs were of many different animals. Much of what I saw was indescribable. Some of the most hideous creatures one can imagine dwell in hell. And then I saw Satan. He was very tall and ugly. He had a spear in his hands that was dripping with blood, and he tried to capture me but he was unable to come near me. All he could do was stare at me because I was being protected by the Spirit of the Living God. Psalms 46:1 says, "God is our refuge and strength, a very present help in trouble."

I started to scream and I said, "Lord, please take me from this place." At this time tears began to flow from my eyes like rain falling from the sky. I was in great torment.

It was at this time that the Spirit of God said to me, "If you do not do better, this is where you would come." And suddenly my spirit came back into my body in the ICU.

Early that Sunday morning on January 7, 1989, after I had regained consciousness, I heard a still small voice say to me, "Everything is going to be all right." I looked all around to see where this voice came from, but there was no one in the room. I knew then that it was the voice of God. Suddenly I felt a peace that I cannot describe come over my being. Philippians 4:7 says, "And the peace of God, which passeth all understanding, shall keep your hearts and minds through Christ Jesus."

After I regained consciousness, I realized that I was still connected to a life support machine and many tubes were still connected to my body. Eventually the nurses came into the ICU and saw that I was awake. They ran and called the doctors, and when they came, I could tell by their faces that they were amazed that I had come back from the dead. I had been to hell and now I was back. Give God praise and glory. I was then taken from the ICU and placed back into male medical ward 1. While in the ward, the nurses came and removed the life support machine and the last two tubes from my stomach, and they cleaned me up. I can truly thank God and say that I have never had tubes on any part of my body from that day to now. Thank you, Jesus.

That Sunday evening two missionary sisters were praying and witnessing on my ward, and they came to my bedside and asked if I was saved, and I said no. One of the sisters asked me if I knew that Jesus can save and heal me. And I said yes. At this time I was in extreme pain and they asked if I am ready to give my life to the Lord, and I said yes, so they had me repeat the sinner's prayer and I said, "Lord Jesus, come into my life and be my Savior." And suddenly I felt God's presence come over me, and my life was never the same again. Psalms 16:11 says, "In thy presence is fulness of joy; at thy right hand there are pleasures for evermore."

The missionaries left the ward, and I kept repeating these words: "Lord, thank you for healing me." And suddenly the power of the Living God fell on me, and I jumped out of the bed, shouting as I gave God thanks and praise.

The nurses ran back to my bed and asked, "What is wrong with you? We've just removed these tubes from you." In other words they were trying to tell me that I was not well, but I knew that God had healed me because I felt brand-new. 2 Corinthians 5:17 says, "Therefore if any man be in Christ, he is a new creature old things are passed away; and behold, all things, are become new."

The following day the hospital attendants took me to be x-rayed, and when the doctors got the results a little later that day, they could not find anything wrong with me. They were again amazed and I started to cry. The Lord spoke to me and said, "When you were in your mother's womb, I chose you to be and end-time prophet, to let my people know that hell is real, and you shall lay hands on the sick and they shall recover." I was released from the hospital three days later, and when I went home and when my family members saw me, they were amazed and said that I was a walking miracle. I can honestly say that I have not been admitted to a hospital from then to now, and when I do go, it is only for checkups.

At eighteen years old I answered the call of God. From that time on I began preaching the Gospel of Jesus Christ with signs and wonders following and laying hands on the sick and seeing them recover. In Mark 16:17–18 Jesus said that "these signs shall follow them that believe; In my name shall they cast out devils; they shall speak with new tongues; They shall take up serpents; and if they drink any deadly thing, it shall not hurt them; they shall lay hands on the sick, and they shall recover."

Whatever you are going through in life, especially if you are not a child of God and you are bound by sin, God is able to deliver you from sin and set you free. Jesus said in John 10:10, "The thief cometh not, but for to steal, and to kill, and to destroy: I am come that they might have life, and that they might have it more abundantly."

Do not worry about what people might say. Everybody has to stand before God and give an account for what they have done in this life. 2 Corinthians 5:10 says, "For we must all appear before the judgment seat of Christ; that every one may receive the things done in his body, according to that he hath done, whether it be good or bad." You are special. Do not be like me; I had to learn the hard way. Hell is no place to go. The Bible says it is a place of eternal torment (Luke 16:23).

Jesus said in Mathew 16:26, "For what is a man profited, if he shall gain the whole world, and lose his own soul? or what shall a man give in exchange for his soul?"

Ministers, if you have slackened your ride with God or are in a backslidden condition, get back up, dust yourself off, and keep running for Jesus. Proverbs 24:16 says, "For a just man falleth seven times, and riseth up again: but the wicked shall fall into mischief." If you are not serving God, you are serving the devil. Satan does not love you and only wants to destroy you. He knows what it is to serve God, and he does not want you to have that wonderful experience. Satan does not want you to go to heaven; he wants you to go to hell. Do not sell your soul to the devil for power or wealth. It is not worth it. If you are looking for the right way, come to Jesus. Jesus said in John 14:6, "I am the way, the truth, and the life: no man cometh unto the Father, but by me." John 10:1 says, "He that entereth not by the door into the sheepfold, but climbeth up some other way, the same is a thief and a robber." If you look at what is happening in the world today, we can surely see that the imminent return of our Lord is near, so let us prepare to meet our God.

If you have not given your heart to the Lord, this is a wonderful time to do it. Just say this prayer: Heavenly Father, in the name of your Son, Jesus, I ask that you come into my life, to be my Lord and Savior. I ask that you cleanse me from every sin, for I believe that Jesus Christ died on Calvary's cross for my sins, and I believe that he arose from the dead and is seated on the right hand of the Father and is making intercession for me right now. Thank you, Jesus, for coming into my heart and being my Lord and Savior. I promise to serve you all my days. Amen.

Congratulations and welcome to the family of God.

Hell Is Real (Part 2)

It was at 3:30 a.m. on Friday, June 6, 2009. While staying at my friends in Pastor Alvin Davis's house, I made my second visit into hell. Can you believe that after twenty-one years the Lord took me in a vision back into hell? Let me just remind my readers that hell is real, and it is the place and destination of people who do not accept Jesus Christ as their Lord and Savior or serve him while they were here on earth. It was about twelve thirty on Friday when I went to bed, with nothing in particular on my mind, and certainly I was not thinking about taking another trip into hell. At about three thirty, the Lord took me into a vision where Pastor Alvin Davis and I were sitting on the back porch of this home that overlooked a graveyard. Pastor Davis asked, "Prophet, can you see that spirit coming out of the graveyard?"

I asked, "Where is he?"

And Pastor Davis said, "I see him coming out the tomb and he is wretched."

I could not see him, but I could smell him and he smelled awful. And suddenly I was transported from the porch into this dark place, and it was extremely hot and worms were everywhere. I then knew I was back in hell. I then saw hooded demons with worms coming out from every part of their bodies imaginable, and they were lined up on both sides of the street. I saw liquid fire, and there were tunnels where I heard many screams, and I then went to the left of the street into tunnel where I heard the screams. As I entered, I heard a female's voice saying, "Help me, help me." I continued to follow the screams until I saw this lady, and her body was infested with worms, and when she saw me, she said, "Please, please, please, give me some water. I am thirsty and tell my family not to come here to take me from this place." After witnessing the state of this woman, I became terrified. As I continued through the tunnel, I saw two demons that were about eight feet tall. One of them had the face of a ram and the other the face of a horse. They both had human bodies, but the horse-head had human feet. Both had thick spears, which were about five feet long, and they were dripping with blood. These demons were hideous and intimidating, and they were standing guard at this gate. Hot lava came down into the tunnel from everywhere. And as I approached the gate, it opened on its own accord, and as I passed the demons, they just stared menacingly, and I was drenched in sweat because it was extremely humid and hot.

After entering the gate, I heard what sounded like thousands upon thousands of screams, and when I looked around, I saw an innumerable amount of souls screaming and crying and the demons continuously tortured these souls with what appeared to be pitchforks that were about six feet long. As I continued on, many of the souls that saw me cried "Help me, help me" as worms continued to engulf their flesh, and my heart became overwhelmed with grief and I started to cry because of the torment and excruciating agony that these souls were experiencing. I realized that there was no hope or redemption for these souls for they were eternally damned. And even throughout all of this, the demons seemed to sadistically enjoy inflicting pain on these souls, and they laughed continuously as they did it. They also looked at me and I could see the deep-seated hatred in their menacing eyes, but I thank God for his Holy Spirit, for they could not touch me because I was protected by the omnipotent and omnipresent one. No wonder David said in Psalms 139:7–10, "Whither shall I go from thy spirit? or whither shall I flee from thy presence? If I ascend up into heaven, thou art there: if I make my bed in hell, behold, thou art there. If I take the wings of the morning, and dwell in the uttermost parts of the sea; even there shall thy hand lead me, and thy right hand shall hold me."

My brothers and sisters, God is sovereign; he is in control not only of the physical earth but of the entire universe; he is in control of not only the physical world but also the spiritual world. He's Lord of heaven and he's Lord of hell, and he made it as a place of punishment for the devil and his angels.

As I continued through the tunnel, I saw twelve hooded demons around a circular table, and their faces amazed me. They were chanting in their own language, which I could not understand. One had the head of a fly; another had the head of a goat; one had the head of a snake, with human eyes that were bloodshot; one had the head of an octopus; three had human faces; and the other five had kangaroo-shaped heads. Instead of fingers, they had claws, and worms were oozing from their bodies.

As I journeyed on, I constantly heard cries of "Help me, help me." As I walked, I heard the voice of a woman and she was screaming, "No, no!" and she said, "I did not mean to hurt those people. I did not mean to put my hands in that stuff." As I drew closer, I saw this woman in a cell to the left, and she was disfigured and worms were coming from every part of her body, and as she held her head up, she kept saying, "This is not right. Warn the others and tell them not to come to this place."

As I continued on, I came to the end of this tunnel and it opened into a wide area. I again saw an incalculable amount of souls, and they were saying, "No, no, no, help me, help me, help me," and it got louder each time. And fire was all around and throughout the people. The suddenly I saw four creatures that from the waist up had the appearance of crocodiles and from the waist down had human bodies and hooked crocodiles' tails. Two of the creatures were black and two were red, with all having one eye in the middle of each of their foreheads, and their hands were webbed and looked like fins. As they stared and pointed at me, I made a hasty retreat and I walked out of that tunnel as fast as I could, and I found myself back on the main street of hell. As I journeyed on, I observed that the road was very long and wide, and there was an arch of fire that stretched the length and width of the road. There appeared to be many prison cells with iron bars on each side of the road. I also heard the screams of the damned from behind these bars, but I could not see them.

As I continued, I heard a loud sound that sounded like metals grinding against each other and I was sweating profusely. I then came to an area where there were huge rocks that were covered with worms on both sides of the street, and the stench of rotting flesh filled the air. As I passed, I heard many demons laughing, and it sounded like "Ha, ha, ha, ha, ha, ha, ha." I picked up my pace and I heard the Spirit of God say "Relax" and I slowed down. As I continued on the road of hell, I looked in the distance and I saw hundreds of gates that were about nine feet high, and this appeared to be a main checkpoint of hell. And as I approached the gates, they opened simultaneously and demons came out of each gate. They all had human heads with donkeys' ears and horses' bodies, and they had worms coming from their bodies and falling into their hands—I mean, claws. Half were red, half were black, and they smelled terrible. As I reached within twenty feet of these creatures, they looked at each other and afterward stared menacingly at me, but that was all that they could do because I was protected by the Spirit of the Living God.

I was not allowed to go through those gates and afterward took a left turn off the main road and went into another tunnel. I saw many caves on each side of the road, and I also heard many screams and voices saying, "Lord, give me another chance." As I continued on, I came to a huge gate that was guarded closer to the gate. The guards moved to the other side, and the gate opened. As I walked through, I saw molten fire on each side of the road, and I heard many screams. And as I journeyed on, I came to four gates; two appeared to be about fifteen feet high and two about twenty feet high, and all were about ten feet apart. As I came to the first gate, I saw two demons that were about eight feet tall, and they had full eyes that were red like fire, their faces were like the faces of the gremlins in the movies, and their coats, which stretched to the ground, were black. And they stared at me for about five minutes, then backed on the side. The gate opened and I walked through the inside of the gate. As I walked through, I saw two hooded demons that had coats that stretched to the length of their bodies, and they had thick belts around their waists. Thorns appeared to be sticking from their shoulders, and they carried swords that were five feet long and very thick. And these swords appeared to be very hot because they were glowing, and smoke and blood were coming from their swords. I was astonished at what I saw.

As I proceeded, I saw molten fire everywhere and I heard man's screams. As I continued, the road suddenly opened wide and I saw literally thousands upon thousands of people (souls), and they were crying, reaching, and saying, "Sir, help me, please help me. Take me from this place." They were surrounded by demons who had pitchforks in their hands, and they were taunting, laughing at, and tormenting them continuously. The demons also stared at each other, then menacingly at me as if they wanted to grab me, but they could not because I was protected by the Spirit of the Living God. At this time I was sweating because it was extremely hot, and I was so afraid that my heart also became full, and I began to cry because I realized that those people were in a state of hopelessness. I turned around and got out of that tunnel as fast as I could, and I came out the first gate.

I saw the second gate and it was guarded by two demons whose heads and bodies were like that of dinosaurs, but they had human hands and feet but with dinosaur tails. They were about ten feet tall, and they had pitchforks that had six prongs on each end. Worms were also coming from their bodies and they smelled stinky. They stared menacingly at me, and I started to vomit. As I entered the gate, I saw steam coming from the gates. I also heard loud noises that sounded like "Ha, ha, ha, ha, ha, ha, ha." I saw molten fire everywhere. As I passed through the gate, I looked back and up and I saw a demon on the second story of the gate, and he was very thick and had one eye and he appeared to be the guard on watch. In his hand he had a chain that was about seven feet long and on its end it had a ball with spikes. As I looked forward, I saw many hooded demons in a circle, and in the middle of the circle, I saw signs and drawings on the ground that appeared to be demonic in nature. The demons were dancing and chanting in a language that I could not understand. For a few minutes I just stared in amazement, and after regaining my composure, I continued walking. I began to ascend some steps that were about fifteen steps in total. And as I came to the end of the steps, I looked down and saw and open trench with smoke ascending from it. I was unable to cross, but I looked ahead and I saw fire everywhere and enumerable souls screaming and saying, "God, please give me another chance or let me go and warn my family about this place." I saw worms just eating away their flesh, and as fast as the souls scratched themselves, their skin grew back. I turned around and walked back down the steps and went out the second gate.

As I approached the third gate, I saw two demons with their backs to me. When they turned around, I saw that they had the appearance of scorpions. Their heads were hooded, but I saw their eyes and they were green. They had scorpion tails and were about ten feet tall (the third gate was about twenty feet high), and they stared menacingly at me for what appeared to be about ten minutes. I was afraid because I did not know their intentions, and finally they backed on the side, and as I entered through the third gate, I heard the screams of a lady coming from my right side, and she was saying, "No, no, no, no, don't do this to me. Lord, please give me another chance." Afterward I heard the laughter of what I suspected to be a demon because I did not see him but I heard him laugh loudly: "Ha, ha, ha, ha, ha, ha, ha, ha." I continued on. I came to an archway that appeared to lead directly into a semicircular building that stretched for miles. As I entered, I saw a circular rock building that stretched for miles. As I entered, I saw a circular rock that had a circumference of about twenty feet, and it was suspended about seven feet in midair—I mean, midhell. On top of this was a chair made of stone, and sitting in this chair was a huge demon that had a ram's horn on top of his head, and he was dressed completely in black. About six feet in front on the left side of the demon in the chair, I saw a hideous, disfigured, and thick demon who stood about eight feet tall, and he had what appeared to be a javelin in his hand. I saw two snakelike demons who had two heads each on the immediate left and right of the demon in the chair. I perceived that this demon in the chair was one which had position and power in the kingdom of darkness. I was astonished and dumbfounded at what I had seen for what appeared to be about three minutes. When I came to myself and my senses I heard multitudes of people crying and screaming, but I did not see them. At this time I began to sweat profusely. I was frightened, nervous, and amazed at what I was experiencing, and even though the Holy Spirit was with me, I was still allowed to experience the overwhelming terror, heat, and helplessness of the eternally damned.

I continued on and I saw caves on both sides of the road, and after passing the caves, I saw molten fire on both sides of the road, and worms were everywhere. Suddenly I saw twelve imps, or short demons, in a circle and they were chanting to each other in a language I did not understand. They wore hooded garments and I could not see their faces. They turned toward me and they opened their circle. I walked through as fast I could, and I continued to look back as they closed circle. As I turned back around and continued forward, I heard loud sounds like "Ching, ching, ching, ching, ching" and then laughter, "Ha, ha, ha, ha, ching, ching." And I beheld a huge, hideous demon-like beast who had six eyes and many horns on his head, and a thick chain was around his neck and it was long and fastened to a rock. He also had six legs and they looked like the tentacles of an octopus. Worms were coming from his body, and blood was dripping from his mouth. He stared at me, and after seeing this, I ran back out the third gate as fast as I possibly could.

After exiting the third gate, I saw four demons that stood in my path as I made my way toward the fourth gate. Two were on each side of the road, one in front and the other about six feet back. They appeared to be about eight feet tall and were bent from the waist down, and they had hoofed feet, and from the waist up they had human bodies. Their faces were hooded but had the shape of dog faces. They also had long spears in their hands. After seeing these creatures, I was amazed, and the only words I could say were "Oh my God." They smelled awful and I had to place my hand over my mouth and nose as I passed. The first two demons stayed in their positions, but as I got within eight feet of the last two demons, they came together and looked at each other and then looked at me, and I wondered what they were thinking, and suddenly they backed on the side and I very quickly passed.

As I continued toward the fourth gate, I saw two other creatures in front of the gate that appeared to be eight feet tall and had four eyes, two in the front and two in the back of their heads. They had six human arms, with three on each side of their bodies. They both had human bodies, but their heads had the appearance of rhinoceroses' heads.

I want to interject and say that many of these creatures that I saw I am trying to describe to the best of my ability. I have never seen or have known of any creatures on earth such as these. I stood amazed at what I was seeing. I kept rubbing my eyes and pinching myself to see if what I was experiencing was real. These creatures had holes in their bodies, and worms were coming from every part. I was also sweating profusely because I was extremely hot.

As I reached the two demons, they backed on the side and the fourth gate opened automatically. I saw molten fire everywhere. I also heard the deafening sounds of the screams and cries of millions of men's souls, and they were saying, "Oh, Lord, give me another chance, please stop, stop." My heart became full and I began to cry because I heard these men crying and asking for help, and I could not help because they were lost forever. I also heard the reverberating sound of "Doom, doom, doom, doom" and laughter, "Ha, ha, ha, ha, ha," everywhere. I tried but could not discern where the sounds and laughter were coming from. I was so afraid, I began to run not out the gate but deeper beyond the fourth gate.

Then I heard the voice of God say, "Stop, what are you running for?"

I stopped suddenly and I had to go back to where I began running because I missed what God wanted to show me. As I continued on, suddenly I came to a trench that was about three feet deep and one hundred feet long. It was filled with fire, and fire supernaturally parted and allowed me to walk through. After coming out of the trench, I heard chanting. As I continued on the road of hell, I saw on the left side of the road a room filled with demons who had many different features and sizes, and they were chanting in a language I did not understand.

As I journeyed on, I came to a toll booth or checkpoint in the middle of the street, and a demon was inside on the left side of the booth. He opened the right side and I walked through. As I continued on, I heard many screams, and worms were everywhere. I came to a huge brick door that opened into a building in the middle of the road. The door opened and I went through. It was dark and I could see no one, but I felt the demons in different areas of this building. I made a left turn in the building, and I heard screams and cries even though I did not see anyone. I somehow knew souls were being tormented because fire was everywhere. Suddenly I saw a three-headed demon that had one eye in the middle of each of his head. He had many horns, and he stood about ten feet tall, and he had six imps, three on each side of his shoulder, and they appeared to be about one foot tall. He had about eight tentacles as legs, and he had a tail that had a hooked shape and many thorns. This demon was bound by four thick chains (two on his front legs and two on his back legs), and his movement was limited. He had an iron ornament around his neck with demonic signs and skulls as engravings. As he stared at me, I stared back at him. I was amazed and afraid, and the imps on his shoulders were laughing and jumped from one shoulder to another. This demon was red as fire, and his body was full of scales.

As I regained my composure, I moved to the opposite side of the street and continued on my journeyed through hell. I would like to mention at this time that the many scenes that I am describing are on the streets of hell, and the gates are on the streets of hell and are guarded by demons, and there is no easy access for tormented souls from one area to the other. I thank God for his Holy

Spirit, who was with me and allowed me to travel past these gates and into the middle of a crater. Off to the right side in the distance, molten lava was coming out of the top of the hill and flowing down the sides. Strangely this appeared to be a beautiful sight. However, I had to make haste because the area was extremely hot and I was sweating like crazy, so I ran with my head down.

As I continued on, I heard many screams. I stopped suddenly and raised my head, and I saw the souls of the damned in the fire, and I also saw many demons rejoicing and dancing over the lost souls in the fire. I then heard two of the demons say, "See, you should have listened to the Christians, but no, you were greedy and wanted to go after the things of the world. This is what you get for not listening." And they laughed. My brothers and sisters, I'm reminded of other word of God in 1 John 2:15–17, which says, "Love not the world, neither the things that are in the world. If any man love the world, the love of the Father is not in him. For all that is in the world, the lust of the flesh, and the lust of the eyes, and the pride of life, is not of the Father, but is of the world. And the world passeth away, and the lust thereof: but he that doeth the will of God abideth for ever." These demons were about ten feet tall and had human bodies, but their eyes and heads were like that of a pig. They had snouts and rams' horns were on their heads.

After seeing the lost souls and hearing the demons, my heart became full and I began to cry and I said, "Enough is enough, I can't take it anymore." Suddenly I was back in my body and in my room. Then I heard the Spirit of the Lord say to me, "Hell is real, part 2."

As I started to walk toward the fifth gate, I heard a lot of screaming, and liquid fire and worms were everywhere. I saw these two-headed demons standing at the gate. They were ten feet tall, and worms were coming out of their bodies, and they had pickaxes in their hands, each about six feet long, and they started looking at me. I continued walking to the gate. The gate was about fifteen feet tall, and smoke was coming out of the gate. I was amazed when I saw the size and the length of the gate. The demons moved on the side and the gate opened on its own accord, and I went into the gate. I saw this large chair in a rock. A demon sat on the chair, and liquid fire was all around him. He started to look at me and his face was shaped like a frog. He started pointing his fingers at me and he laughing "Ha, ha, ha, ha." I heard people screaming and saying, "Let me go, I don't want to be here. Please do not poke me with that fork." I continued to walk through until I saw little demons poking the people, and the demons stopped and looked at me, and they started talking to each other in their own language, whispering. The smoke was around the people, and they looked at me, stretching their hands toward me and crying, saying, "Help us, give us some water to drink, and tell our family and friends, do not come here." They started grabbing their faces, and I saw worms going through their flesh. I started to cry because their souls are lost forever, and I was sweating a lot.

I walked through I saw these separate cave with people in there, and they started to cry when they saw me and these demons were guiding these caves. As the Spirit of the Lord took me through, all I could smell was rotten flesh and I heard screaming of the lost souls. Suddenly I turned around and went out of the fifth gate.

I found myself on this road walking. On each side of the road were liquid fire and many caves. I started walking fast on the road in front of me. I saw these demons holding hands in a circle, and they were chanting and dancing. I stopped for a few minutes and watched them dancing, and they turned around and look at me. They moved out of the road, and I started to walk toward them and they let me through. I saw this large door, so huge, and the demons were in front of the door. Their faces were like that of horses; their waist down was human and their bodies were full of holes, and smoke was coming from their mouths. And I said to myself, "What kind of stuff is this?" Each one of them had a spear, and blood was dripping from it. These demons were about eight feet tall, and when they saw me, they moved on the side of the door, and the door opened on its own accord.

When I got in the door, I saw these other demons with hoofed legs, and their hands were like claws. They started laughing, saying in a strange voice, "Why did you come here?" They smelled so awful, but I didn't answer them back. So I continued walking through the door. Worms were everywhere, and these worms were three inches long. I heard the people screaming, saying, "Help me, help me, help me, somebody help me." My heart went out for them, but I could not help them.

As the Spirit of the Lord took me through, I came to the sixth gate, and I saw a big rock in front of the gate, and screams were coming from this rock, and I asked myself why the rock was in front of the gate. I started to walk toward the gate. All I heard were creeping sounds and was started to get frightened. I said to myself, "The Lord did not give the spirit of fear, but love and power and a sound mind." I kept on walking toward the gate. All of a sudden the big rock moved on the side on its own accord, and the gate opened and I went in. I saw these two ladies in a cell, saying to each other, "If we did know this, what we were doing to each other was wrong."

I said to myself, "What are they talking about?"

The Spirit of the Lord said to me that they were in relationship with each other; they were lesbians, and they were rubbing their bodies for they were tormented. They looked at me and said, "Please warn the people this is not right."

All of a sudden this demon appeared to their cell and said to them, "I know it is not right, but you want to go with women and not men." And the demon started laughing at them.

As the Spirit of the Lord walked me through the gate, I saw six demons; three were on my right side and three were on my left side. Two were snakelike from their heads to their waists and humanlike from waist down, and the third one had a tiger-like head and his hands and legs were human. The other three were hooded demons, and I could not see their faces. They were dressed in black, and their hands were just bones. All six of them had spears in their hands, and steam was coming from each spear. And they looked at me in an angry way for a few minutes, and they started chanting and singing and hitting the spears on the ground. As I walked through and looked around, I saw this tall ladder in a form of a rock, and on top of it was this ugly beast. He was guiding the gate, and worms were just crawling on the ladder up and down by the hundreds. And I just kept on walking through, and I heard the sound of prison cells hitting together, saying, "Bang, bang, bang, bang, bang, bang," and I heard the people crying, saying, "Help us, help us, for we are tormented in this flame. Please help us, please help us." And I heard the demons started laughing at the people, saying, "There is no way out, ha, ha, ha, ha, he, he, he." I said to myself, "Oh my Lord, what a bad state to be in."

As I walked through, I came to this dark tunnel and I said, "I am not going inside that dark tunnel."

The Spirit of the Lord said to me, "Go in, I am with you."

I went in and could not see anything. I even could not see myself. As the Spirit of the Lord took me through, I heard this loud sound saying, "Doom, doom, doom." The deeper I went in the tunnel, the louder it got. Suddenly I saw fire everywhere and I saw the demon was beating this drum, and he was sitting on this rock. When I looked on the other side on my left, I saw these small demons; they were sitting around the fire and they started laughing. I saw people inside the fire screaming, and their flesh came out of their bodies, and the more they scratched, the more flesh came. Worms were going through their bodies, and their eyes were opening up wide, and when they saw me, they said, "Could you tell our family and friends, do not come to this place for we are tormented in this place." The demons turn around and looked at me, and they stopped laughing for a few minutes. Their faces were that of oxen, and worms were coming from their bodies. They began laughing again.

As the Holy Spirit walked me through, I saw this demon. He had four wings and was ten feet tall, and in his hand was a knife. He took the knife and licked it with his tongue. His eyes were red and his feet were hoofed. Suddenly his wings started to move, and then I stood still for a minute to see what he was going to do. His wings started moving fast, and he lifted off the ground and flew to the other side of the gate. I was amazed to see what just happened, and I began to walk. I saw three prison gates in midair and fire was all around them. As I walked through, I saw these black coffins and fire was underneath them, and suddenly I found myself out of the sixth gate.

And the Holy Spirit took me through the other part of hell, and he said to me, "You are going to gate 7."

Suddenly I saw the seventh gate from afar. Before I reached to the gate, I saw four demons. Two were on each side. The demon on my right, the first one, had a lion's body from the waist down, and his upper body was human. He had in his hand a bow and arrows. The second one was half-horse and half-human, and in his hand was a long spear. On the left, the other two was ten feet tall and thick, and they had hats on their heads, and their faces were disfigured. Worms came from their bodies and they smelled stinky and in their hands was a spear. I passed through them and I went through the seventh gate. I saw a lot of arches everywhere, and liquid fire and smoke rained down the arches. I saw boiling hole with fire inside, and I saw different caves, and these caves had locks on them. As I walked through I saw this demon sitting on a rocking chair. His head was shaped like a dog's face and his body was shaped in human form. He had some keys in his hand. His toes were curled up like bird feet. He looked at me in a strange way, and on his head was a crown, and on his right side was a cobra with two heads. On the left side of the chair was a short demon.

As I walked through, I saw this carriage and in the carriage was a beast, and he's chanting. After that I saw the demons dancing and jumping around the fire, and their hands were lifted up. They were worshipping in their own way. As I journeyed, I heard a male voice saying, "Help me, help me, please someone help me. I had enough. Give me some water please. I am tormented and I didn't mean to go with the little baby." When I heard what that man was saying, it hurt me deeply. Mathew 18:6 says, "But whoso shall offend one of these little ones which believe in me, it were better for him that a millstone were hanged about his neck, and that he were drowned in the depth of the sea." As I journeyed on, I saw this demon with four hands, and he was putting some substance inside the fire. His head was that of a goat and on top of his head were three long horns. He was eight feet tall and he was red. And he had a long tail with spikes on it, and when he saw me, he stopped working for a few minutes. He started grunting—"Grunt, grunt, grunt"—and smoke was coming out of his nose. He turned around and started working again. As I walked through, I saw this other beast with six legs. He was ten feet tall, and his head was that of a human. His hair was very long, and I stood still for a few minutes looking at this beast with amazement, and there were four thick chains tied to him, and he looked at me in an angry way, and blood was dripping from his mouth. I said to myself, "Oh my Lord, what kind of beast is he?" Liquid fire was everywhere.

I started walking to in the deeper parts of hell. I heard loud laughing, and I couldn't describe the laughing; it was very scary sound. I saw prison gates around, and suddenly I found myself out of the seventh gate back on the road into the deeper part of hell. As I was walking, I saw this tunnel, and out of this tunnel was liquid fire coming out of it. I heard people saying, "Please, please take these worms out. They are eating our flesh. Please help us." The people started crying and screaming, and the demons started laughing.

As I journeyed on, I came to this next gate, which was the eighth gate. Two demons were guarding it. They were seven feet tall and they had bows and arrows in their hands. Their heads were like ape heads and their bodies were like human bodies. They had one eye in the middle of each of their foreheads. The demons moved from the front of the gate. It opened on its own accord, and I went into the gate. I saw eight demons talking to each other, saying, "Let us go on earth to get some more people to destroy them."

One of the demons said, "Let each one take one."

The rest of the demons agreed. One said, "I will destroy their marriage."

The second one said, "I will cause them to take drugs."

The third one said, "I will cause the people to steal."

The fourth said, "I will cause them to kill."

The fifth said, "I will go into the church and deceive the people."

The sixth one said, "I will give them power of things."

The seventh one said, "I will be the seaside."

The eighth one said, "Lesbians," and they started laughing.

People inside them crying and screaming, saying, "Let me out, let me out of this place for I am tormented in this flame." They were putting their hands through the bars, and the bars were locked and at every bar were a demon and the demon's aid. There was no way out, and each demon had a pitchfork in their hands, and blood was dripping from the pitchfork. All of a sudden the demons started chanting and laughing. They had different sizes and different shapes. They were too many for me to describe.

As I journeyed on, I smelled the scent of rotten flesh. It was very stinky. I saw demons flying from one side of the gate to the other side of the gate. I saw two demons with four eyes; two were in the front and two were in the back of their heads. They were six feet tall. I stood still in amazement. They had pitchforks in their hands. As I passed by the demons, they just stared menacingly. I was drenching in sweat because it was extremely humid and hot. I came to this tunnel, and two demons were guarding the tunnel. They were seven feet tall, had hands like crab claws, and had human bodies, and worms were coming out of their bodies. They had spears in their hands and they moved in front of the tunnel. I went in and again saw and incalculable amount of souls, and they were saying, "No, no, help me, help me." It got louder each time and fire was all around and through the people.

Then I saw two beasts with four heads. Their bodies were animal bodies. One was brown and one was black. They were five feet tall. As I continued through the tunnel, I saw six hooded demons on top of a rock, and they were chanting, which I could not understand. One had the head of an elf, one had the head of a tiger, one had the head of a frog, and one had the head of a cat, and the others had human faces, and worms were oozing from their bodies.

As I journeyed on, I constantly heard cries of "Help me, help me." As I walked, I heard the voice of demons chanting. As I got closer, I saw the demons kneeling down in a circle with their faces to the ground. They all were wearing black, and they were stinky. Suddenly I turned around and walked back down to the tunnel and went out of the eighth gate.

As I journeyed on the road of hell, I arrived at the ninth gate. I saw one demon with his back to me. When he turned around, I saw that he had the appearance of a human, and his face was full of holes, and worms were all over his face. He was about twelve feet tall. The ninth gate was about twenty feet high, and he stared menacingly at me for what appeared to be about ten minutes and finally backed on the side. As I entered through the ninth gate, I heard again screams of souls coming from the right side and in the left they were saying "Help me, help me." Worms continued to engulf their flesh. My heart became overwhelmed with grief, and I started to cry because of the torment and excruciating agony that these souls were experiencing. I realized that there was no hope or redemption for these souls for they were eternally damned. Even throughout all of this, I saw the demons seemed to sadistically enjoy inflicting pain on these souls, and they laughed continuously as they did it. They also looked at me and I could see the deep-seated hatred in their menacing eyes.

As I journeyed on, I saw this demon with a spider body and a human head, and he had three horns on his head, and three long teeth came out of his mouth. Two holes were in both sides of his jaw, and he had a spear in his hands. He was about eight feet tall, and worms were coming out of his body. This demon was hideous and intimidating, and he was just there laughing.

Hot lava was coming down the tunnel from everywhere.

As I journeyed on, again I saw fire everywhere and enumerable souls screaming and saying "God, give me another chance" or "Let me warn my family and friends about this place." I saw worms just eating away their flesh. As fast as the souls scratched themselves, their skin grew back. I started to cry because of the torment and excruciating agony that these souls were experiencing. I realized that there was no hope or redemption for these souls for they were eternally damned. I heard the demons laughing, saying, "Ha, ha, ha, ha." As I continued, I heard a loud sound that sounded like prison cells hitting against each other. Again I was sweating profusely, and again I then came to another area where there were huge rocks that were covered with worms on both sides of the street. The stench of rotting flesh filled the air. As I passed, I heard many demons laughing, and it sounded like "He, he, heh, ahahahaha." Again I picked up my pace and I heard the Spirit of God say, "Relax." I slowed down.

As I continued on the road of hell, I looked in the distance and I saw many souls, and they were screaming and crying, saying, "Give me some water please for I am tormented in this flame." Again I started to cry because of the torment and agony that these souls were experiencing.

As I journeyed on, I saw these three creatures that were about ten feet tall. They had eight legs and they had six eyes and four horns on their heads and four sharp teeth coming out of their mouths and blood draining out of their mouths. The three creatures had different colors; one was black, the second one was brown; and the last one was red. They had fish scales all over their bodies, and they were chained to these huge rocks. Worms were coming out of their bodies. They stared menacingly at me, and I was amazed in what I saw. I said to myself, "Oh, Lord, what kind of creatures are these?"

As I journeyed on, again I also heard loud noises that sounded like "Dong, dong, dong," and then I heard laughter that sounded again like "Ha, ha, ha."

I saw molten fire everywhere, and I started sweating again because it was extremely hot. As I journeyed on, suddenly I saw again twelve short demons in a circle, and they were chanting to each other in a language I did not understand. They turned toward me, and they opened their circle. I walk through as fast as I could and I continued to look back as they closed circle. As I turned back around and continued forward, I heard loud sounds again like "Ching, chang, chang" and then laughter, "Ha, ha, hahaha, ching, chang."

Suddenly I found myself out of the ninth gate and made my way toward the tenth gate. As I journeyed onto the tenth gate, I saw three demons that stood in my path. Two was on the right and one was on the left side of the road. One was about eight feet tall and the second was about seven feet tall and the last one was about six feet tall. Their bodies were full of seals, and they had pitchforks in their hands. They had two horns sticking out of their heads, and their ears were sharp and sticky, and their teeth were sticking out of their mouths and their eyes were green. They looked at me in an angry and furious way. They smelled very awful, and I had to place my hand over my mouth and nose. They looked at each other and they looked at me. I wondered what they were thinking. Suddenly they backed on the side, and I very quickly passed.

As I journeyed to the tenth gate, I saw three creatures in front of the gate that were about eight feet tall. They had three eyes, and one of their eyes was on top of their foreheads, and their eyes were green. They had six hands like crab claws. Three were on both sides of their bodies. From the waist down they were humanlike.

Again I wanted to interject and say that many of the creatures that I saw I am trying to describe to the best of my ability. I have never seen or have known of any creatures on earth such as these. I stood amazed at what I was seeing. I kept rubbing my eyes and pinching myself to see if what I was experiencing was real.

As I reached the tenth gate, the gate opened automatically, and I went in and saw fire everywhere. I also heard the sounds of screams and cries of thousands of souls who were saying, "Oh, Lord, give me another chance please. Please stop, stop." My heart got full again and I started to cry because I heard these souls crying and asking for help and I could not help because they were lost forever. Again I also heard the reverberating sound saying like "Doom, doom, doom, doom" everywhere. I tried but could not describe where the sounds were coming from.

As I journeyed through the tenth gate, I saw fire everywhere and five imps, and they were dancing around in this circle, and they were chanting in their own language, but I could not understand them. They were dressed in black with hoods over their heads, and their faces were dark but I could not see their faces because the hoods were over their heads. When they saw me, they stopped dancing and chanting, and I stopped for a few minutes and I could see the deep-seated hatred in their eyes. They opened the circle and they held hands, and they stretched straight across the other side of the gate that I could not pass through the gate. They stayed there for a few minutes just looking at me, and suddenly they went back in a circle and started to dance and start chanting. I went through the gate, but I thank God for his Holy Spirit, for they could not touch me because I was protected by the omnipotent and omnipresent one. No wonder David said in Psalms 139:7–10, "Whither shall I go from thy spirit? or whither shall I flee from thy presence? If I ascend up into heaven, thou art there: if I make my bed in hell, behold, thou art there. If I take the wings of the morning, and dwell in the uttermost parts of the sea; even there shall thy hand lead me, and thy right hand shall hold me."

As I journeyed on, I heard loud screams of the damned coming in front of me, but I could not see them. As I proceeded again, I saw molten fire everywhere, and I heard many screams. As I continued walking through the gate, suddenly the gate of hell enlarged itself wide, and I saw literally thousands upon thousands of souls, and they were crying, reaching, and saying, "Sir, help me, please help me. Take me from this place." They were surrounded by demons who had pitchforks in their hands, and they were tauntingly laughing and tormenting them continuously. The demons also stared at each other, then menacingly at me as if they wanted to grab me, but they could not because I was protected by the Spirit of the Living God. At this time again I was sweating because it was hot, and I was so afraid. My heart also became full, and I began to cry because I realized that these souls were in a state of hopelessness.

As I journeyed on, I saw six demons sitting on this rock table, and they were playing some games with each other, and when they saw me, they got up from the table and they started to speak in their own language, and I could not understand them. Then I stopped for a few minutes, and they started pointing hands at each other, and then they pointed their hands at me. They were about six feet tall, and three of them had heads shaped like squares, and these had one in their forehead. They had no nose and their ears were sharp and sticky, and they had four long teeth were coming out of their mouths, two from the top and two from the bottom. Holes were all throughout their bodies, and worms were just dropping from their bodies. From their shoulders down, they had human bodies, and their toes were like claws. The other three's heads look like horse heads, and they had two eyes but their eyes look like that of a squid; their noses were long, about four inches, and they had two horns on top of their mouths, and worms were all over their faces. From their shoulders down, they had human bodies and their toes were curled up.

Again I want to interject and say that many of these demons and creatures that I saw I am trying to describe to the best of my ability. I have never seen or have known of any creature on earth such as these.

I stood amazed at what I was seeing. Suddenly they started laughing and looking at each other, and they stopped laughing. Afterward they stared menacingly at me, but that was all that they could do because I was protected by the Spirit of the Living God. Psalms 27:1–5 says, "The Lord is my light and my salvation; whom shall I fear? the Lord is the strength of my life; of whom shall I be afraid? When the wicked, even mine enemies and my foes, came upon me to eat up my flesh, they stumbled and fell. Though an host should encamp against me, my heart shall not fear: though war should rise against me, in this will I be confident. One thing have I desired of the Lord, that will I seek after; that I may dwell in the house of the Lord all the days of my life, to behold the beauty of the Lord, and to enquire in his temple. For in the time of trouble he shall hide me in his pavilion: in the secret of his tabernacle shall he hide me; he shall set me up upon a rock."

And after that they went back to the table and sat down. As I continued to walk through, I saw these two trenches that were very long. One was on the right side of the gate and the next one was on the left side of the gate and the next one was on the left side of the gate. When I got closer to the trench, they were very deep and molten fire was in them. I started sweating profusely. Suddenly again I heard what sounded like thousands upon thousands of screams, and when I looked to the right and to the left, I saw an innumerable amount of souls screaming and crying and the demons continuously laughing, saying, "Ha, ha, ha." The demons had pitchforks that were about five feet long, and many of the souls that saw me cried, saying, "Please take me from this place, please take me from this place, please take me from this place, please let me go. Tell my family about this place to come." Worms continued to engulf their flesh, and my heart became overwhelmed with grief, and I started to cry because of the torment and excruciating agony that these souls were experiencing. I realized that there was no hope or redemption for these souls for they were eternally doomed, and even throughout all of this, the demons seemed sadistically enjoy laughing at the souls while they were being tormented. The demons looked at me, and I could see the deep-seated hatred in their menacing eyes, and worms were coming out of the demons.

As I journeyed on and passed the trenches, I saw thousands of worms on both sides of the gate and the stench of rotting flesh filled the air and I put my hands over my mouth and nose for a few minutes till I passed from that area. As I journeyed on, I saw two steps; one was on the right and one was on the left. On top of these steps, I saw two demons. They were about seven feet tall. The first one had a torch in his hands, and the second one had a spear in his hands, and two of them had faces like gremlins. They had one horn on top of their heads and they had two long teeth coming out of their mouths and their eyes were red. From their waist down, they were humanlike, and their feet were like claws. The demons just looked at me and they smelled stinky and I started to vomit. Suddenly when I raised my head to stop vomiting, I saw four short imps that were on a demon. Each one of them had two on their shoulders. I asked myself when these four imps came from. The imps started to chant in their language. As I journeyed on, I heard again loud sounds like "Ching, ching, ching" and then laughter like "Ha, ha, ha, ha, ching, ching." I beheld a large, hideous demon-like snake who had four eyes and many horns on his head and a thick chain around his neck. It was long and fastened to a rock. He also had six legs, and they looked like frog legs. Worms were coming from his body and blood was dripping from mouth. He stared at me, and after seeing this, I stood for a few minutes and I was amazed in what I saw.

As I continued on, suddenly I came to another trench that was about five feet deep and two hundred feet long. It was filled with fire, and the fire supernaturally parted, which allowed me to walk through. After coming out of the trench, I heard again chanting. As I continued on the road of hell, suddenly I saw fire on the road of hell. Suddenly I saw fire everywhere and enumerable souls screaming and saying, "God, please give another chance" or "Let me go and warn my family about this place." I saw worms just eating away their flesh, and as fast as the souls scratched themselves, their skin grew back. My heart became overwhelmed with grief, and I started to cry because of the torment and excruciating agony that these souls were experiencing. I realized that there was no hope or redemption for these souls for they were eternally damned.

As I continued on, I came to an archway that appeared to lead directly into a semicircular building that stretched for miles. As I entered, I saw a rock table. It was suspended about ten feet in midair—I mean, midhell. On top of this table were two imps and their demons, and they were doing some kind of demonic signs with their hands, and they started chanting in their own languages, and I could not understand. The two demons were bent over, and the two imps were dressed in black. On this table were four torches with fire in them, and each one was on the end of each corner of the table. When they saw me, they stopped and they looked at each other, and they looked back at me. I wondered what they were thinking. Worms started to come from their mouths, and they went back and started doing the demonic signs with their hands, and they started chanting in their own language.

As I continued on the road of hell, I saw again on the left side of the road a room filled will demons who had many different features and sizes, and they were chanting in a language I did not understand. As I journeyed on, I came to another tunnel. I walked through and I saw many demons in different areas of this tunnel. I made a right turn in the tunnel, and I heard screams and cries even though I did not see anyone. I somehow thought that souls were being tormented because fire was everywhere.

I would like to mention at this time that the many scenes that I am describing are on the streets of hell and the gates are on the streets of hell and are guarded by demons, and there is no easy access for tormented souls from one area to the other.

As I journeyed on, I heard crying until I saw this man, and his body was infested with worms. When he saw me, he said, "Please, please give me some water. I am thirsty. And tell my family don't come here. Take me from this place." After witnessing the state of this man, I became terrified.

As I continued on I saw two demons that were about nine feet tall. One had the face of a cat and the other had the face of a goat; they both had human bodies. The demon with the cat head had feet that were hoofed, and the demon with goat head had human feet. Both had thick spears that were about seven feet long and were dripping with blood, and worms were oozing out of their bodies see the deep-seated hatred in their menacing eyes and when they saw me and I could see the deep-seated hatred in their menacing eyes.

As I journeyed on the road of hell, I saw again twelve hooded demons around a circular table, and their faces amazed me, and they were chanting in their own language I could not understand, and they just looked at me. As I continued on the road of hell, suddenly I heard screaming and crying of multitudes of people. But I did not see them. At this time I began to sweat profusely, and fire was everywhere. I heard the demons saying to the multitude of people, "See, you should have listened to the Christians, but no, you were greedy and wanted to go after the things of the world. This is what you get for not listening." And they laughed, "Ha, ha, ha, ha, he, he."

As I traveled on, I saw again many demons by the hundreds. Some of which were half-human and half-animal. Their faces, hands, and chests were in human forms, but their thighs and legs were of many different animals. Much of what I saw was indescribable. Some of the most hideous creatures one can imagine dwell in hell. Again I saw Satan and he was very tall and ugly. He had a spear in his hands that was dripping with blood, and he tried to capture me, but he was unable to come near me. All he could do was stare at me because I was being protected by the Spirit of the Living God. Psalms 91:1–3 says, "He that dwelleth in the secret place of the most High shall abide under the shadow of the Almighty. I will say of the Lord, He is my refuge and my fortress: my God; in him will I trust. Surely he shall deliver thee from the snare of the fowler, and from the noisome pestilence." I saw again thousands of souls that were screaming and crying, and at this time, the tears began to flow from my eyes. Suddenly I found myself out of the tenth gate and on the road of hell.

Believe that hell is real, but I come to let you know that I am a living witness. The Spirit of the Living God took me there. Please don't play around with your soul. The Spirit of the Living God said to me, "Let them know that hell is real." If you look at what is happening in the world today, we can surely see the imminent return of our Lord, so let us prepare to meet our God. Satan does not love you. All he wants to do is destroy your soul. If you have not given your heart to the Lord, this is a wonderful time to do it.

As I journeyed on the road of hell, I came to this tunnel and I heard loud sound like "Doom, doom, doom, he, he, he." I went into tunnel and this tunnel had different areas. Liquid fire was everywhere, and I started sweating. Worms were everywhere and the stench of rotting flesh filled the air. As I continued on, again I heard a loud sound that sounded like metals grinding against each other, and then I came to another area where there were huge rocks. Imps were on these rocks, and they were covered with worms and they were jumping from one rock to the other. They were laughing to themselves, and when they saw me, they stopped for a few minutes and they looked at each other. Afterward they stared menacingly at me. As I walked through, they started talking in their own language.

As I walked through the tunnel, suddenly I heard what sounded like thousands upon thousands of screams. When I looked, I saw an innumerable amount souls screaming and crying, and the demons continuously tortured these souls with what appeared to be pitchforks that were about six feet tall. I started to cry because of the torment and the agony that these souls were experiencing. I realized that there was no hope or redemption for these souls for they were eternally damned, and even throughout all of this, the demons seemed to sadistically enjoy inflicting pain on these souls, and they laughed continuously as they did it.

As I continued through the tunnel, I made a right turn to the other part of the tunnel, and suddenly again I heard loud sounds like "Ching, ching, ching" and then laughter, "Ha, ha, ha." I beheld again a huge hideous creature who had three heads and three eyes and many horns on his head, and a thick chain was around his legs fastened to a rock. He also had six legs and they looked like the tentacles of an octopus. Worms were coming from his body and blood was dripping from his mouth. He stared at me, and after seeing this, I was amazed. The only words I could say was "Oh my God." He smelled awful and I had to place my hand over my mouth and nose as I passed him. Suddenly again I also saw many coffins, and in these coffins I saw pastors. How did I know they were pastors? It is because they had their pastor's collars around their necks. I saw the demons strike them with their spears, and I also saw fire under every coffin, and the pastors would scream aloud from the pain that was being inflicted upon them by the demons. I heard the demons say to the pastors, "You should have known better. You were supposed to lead the people to Jesus, but no, you want to go after the things of the world." At this time I started to cry because of the hopeless state of these pastors.

As I traveled on, I saw again demons. Some of which were half-human and half-animal. Their faces, hands, and chests were in human form, but their thighs and legs were of many different animals. The demons started laughing, saying, "Ha, ha, ha." When they saw me, they stopped laughing and they stared at me. I could see the deep-seated hatred in their menacing eyes. As I continued on, I heard screaming and crying of men's souls, saying, "Lord Jesus, give us another chance please. Forgive us for having sex with men." As I came closer, I saw the men and their flesh were coming off their bodies, and they were screaming. Worms were going through their bodies.

In the tunnel, I saw three demons, and when they saw me, they said to me, "Please help us, please." They were stretching their hands toward me as worms continued to engulf their flesh. My heart became overwhelmed with grief, and I started to cry again because of the torment and excruciating agony that these men were experiencing. I realized that there was no hope for these men for they were eternally damned.

As I continued on, I heard demons laughing and chanting at the same time. I took a left turn through another tunnel. Again it was dark and I could see no one, but I felt the demons touching me. As I continued on, I exited the darkness and again I saw many demons in different areas of this tunnel. Suddenly I heard screams and cries. Even though I did not see anyone, I knew souls were being tormented because liquid fire was everywhere. As I journeyed through the tunnel, I saw three demons, and they were across the tunnel with their hands stretched out. They were about eight feet tall, and three of them had different colors, and two of them had human heads and their bodies were that of animals with two legs, and their faces were full of marks, and they had one eye in the middle of their foreheads and their noses were curled up. The third one looked like a gremlin, and worms were coming from every part of his body. I stood still for a few minutes, and when they saw me, I could see the deep-seated hatred in their menacing eyes. Suddenly they started laughing aloud, saying, "Ha, ha, ha, he, he." Worms were everywhere. They stopped laughing and they started breathing fast. They moved from across the tunnel.

As I continued on, again I heard a loud sound that sounded like metals grinding against each other. I was sweating profusely. As I continued through the tunnel, suddenly it opened into a wide area. I again saw an incalculable amount of souls, and they were saying, "No, no, no, help me, help me." It got louder each time, and fire was all around and throughout the people. The demons continuously tortured these souls with pitchforks that were six feet long. Worms continued to engulf their flesh. My heart became overwhelmed with grief, and I started to cry again because of the torment and excruciating agony that these souls were experiencing. I realized that there was no hope or redemption for these souls for they were eternally damned, and even throughout all of this, the demons seemed to sadistically enjoy inflicting pain on these souls, and they laughed continuously as they did it.

As I continued through the tunnel, I saw worms on both sides of the tunnel, and again the stench of rotten flesh filled the air. As I continued on, I heard again many demons laughing and it sounded like "Ha, ha, ha." Again I picked up my pace and I heard the Spirit of the Lord say to me again, "Relax." And I slowed down.

As I continued through the tunnel, I looked in the distance and I saw again many gates that were about nine feet high, and this appeared to be a main checkpoint of hell. As I continued through the tunnel, I saw again many demons. Some of these creatures were half-human and half-animal. Much of what I saw was indescribable. Some of the most hideous creatures one can imagine dwell in hell.

Again I want to interject and say that many of these creatures and demons that I saw I am trying to describe to the best of my ability, and again, I have never seen or known of any creatures on earth such as these. I stood amazed at what was seeing and again. I kept rubbing my eyes and pinching myself to see if what I was experiencing was real.

As I continued through the tunnel, I saw a lot of caves, and people were in the caves. As I passed the caves, the people were scratching themselves, and the more they scratched themselves, the flesh came back on their bodies. Worms were eating all through their bodies. When the people saw me passing by the cave, they started saying to me, "Please, please, please help me, help me." They were shaking the caves and saying again, "Please help me, help me, help me."

As I continued on, I saw again molten fire everywhere, and I heard many screams. As I passed through the tunnel, suddenly again it opened wide, and I saw literally thousands upon thousands of people, and they were crying, reaching, and saying, "Sir, help me, please, help me, take me from this place." They were surrounded by demons who had pitchforks in their hands and they were taunting, laughing, and tormenting them continuously. At that time I was sweating because it was extremely hot. I was so sad and my heart also became full, and I began to cry because I realized that those souls were in a state of hopelessness, and the demons also stared at me menacingly as if they wanted to grab me, but they could not because I was protected by the Spirit of the Living God. No wonder David said in Psalms 91:5–7, "Thou shalt not be afraid for the terror by night; nor for the arrow that flieth by day; nor for the pestilence that walketh in darkness; nor for the destruction that wasteth at noonday. A thousand shall fall at thy side, and ten thousand at thy right hand; but it shall not come nigh thee."

As I continued through the tunnel, I saw six demons and they were kneeling down and they were chanting in their own language. Their hands were lifted up in the air, and they started to breathe fast. They had different colors, and worms were oozing from their bodies. I saw smoke coming from the ground and molten fire on each side of the tunnel. Suddenly again I also heard loud noise that sounded like "Dang, dang, dang" and then laughter that sounded like "He, he, he, he, ha, ha, ha." Worms were everywhere and the stench of rotting flesh filled the air.

As I continued through the tunnel, I started sweating again profusely. I heard the voice of people screaming "No, no," and they said, "I did not mean to hurt those people, I did not mean to put my hands in that stuff." As I drew closer, I saw the people in different cells, and they were disfigured and worms were coming from every part of their bodies. As the people held their heads, they kept saying, "This is not right." When they saw me, they said to me, "Please, sir, warn the people and tell them not to come here."

I want to interject and say to you that hell is real, and it is the destination of people who do not accept Jesus Christ as their Lord and Savior or serve him while they were here on earth. Hell is no place for you to go. In Mark 9:44, Jesus says in hell the worms "dieth not, and the fire is not quenched."

As I continued through the tunnel, I saw this creature. He was very huge and his body was full of scales and his legs were chained down. He had four eyes; two was in the front of his head and two were in the back of his head. He had six horns on his head and his eyes were red and his face was full of scars and his teeth were about four inches long. He had paws on each side of his mouth and blood was dripping from his body. His body had two different colors, red and black, and his nose was long and sharp. His feet were like claws. He was very ugly, and worms were coming from every part of his body. I saw these imps jumping from one part of his body to the other part of his body. And as I continued on, the creatures just stared menacingly, and I was drenched in sweat because it was extremely humid and hot. Suddenly I heard what sounded like thousands upon thousands of souls screaming and crying, saying, "Lord, please, please give me another chance, please. I am tormented in this place." Suddenly, I heard laughing that sounded again like "Ha, ha, hahaha." The souls just was screaming and crying. I began to cry again because I realized that those souls were in a state of hopelessness.

As I continued walking, I began ascending some steps that were about twenty-five in total. As I came to the steps, I saw steam and again loud sounds like "Ching, ching, ching" and then laughter, "Ha, ha, ha, he, he, he." As I journeyed on, I saw again a hill that appeared to be in the middle of a crater off to the right side in the distance, and molten lava was coming out of the top of the hill and flowing down the sides. Strangely this appeared to be a beautiful sight. However, I had to make haste because the area was extremely hot. I began sweating like crazy, so I ran with my head down. Suddenly I stopped running, and as I continued on, I heard many screaming and I saw the souls of the damned in the fire. I also saw many demons rejoicing and dancing over the lost souls in the fire. I then heard the demons say, "See, you should have listened to the Christians, but no, you were greedy and wanted to go after the things of the flesh, and this is what you get for not listening." The demons continuously tortured the souls with what appeared to be pitchforks. As I continued on, many of the souls that saw me cried out, saying, "Sir, give me some water please. Please, sir, give me some water. For I am tormented in this flame." Worms continued to engulf their flesh. I started to cry again because of the torment and agony that these souls were going through. I realized that there was no hope or redemption for these souls for they were eternally damned. And the demons started to laugh continuously at the souls. Suddenly they also looked at me, and I could see the deep-seated hatred in their menacing eyes.

As I continued through the tunnel, I made a right turn and I found myself to the end of this tunnel and again it opened into a wide area. I again saw and incalculable amount of souls, and they were saying "No more, help me, help me, help me." And it got louder each time. Fire was all around and throughout the people. Then suddenly I saw again four creatures that from the waist up had the appearance of crocodiles and from the waist down had human bodies and scorpion tails, and two of the creatures were black and two were brown. All had three eyes and one of the eyes was in the middle of their foreheads, and their hands were crab hands. They stared and pointed at me. Again I made a hasty retreat and I walked out of that tunnel as fast as I could. Suddenly I found myself back on the main street of hell.

As I journeyed on, I observed that the road was very long and wide, and there was an arch of molten fire that stretched the length and width of the road. There appeared to be many prison cells with iron bars on each side of the road, and I also heard again the screams of the damned from behind these bars, but I could not see them. As I continued on the road of hell, I came to this large gate, and the Spirit of the Lord said to me, "This is eleventh gate." I have never seen a gate so huge, and I saw six demons guarding this gate, and they had spears in their hands, and three were in front of the gate and three were by the side of the gate. They were very ugly and they had different colors; two were black and two were red and the other two were green. Their ears were sharp and stingy, and they had three eyes and the next eye was in their foreheads. Their faces were full of scars. Worms were coming from every part of their bodies, and they smell very bad. I had to put my hands over my nose and mouth. They stared at me and I could see the deep-seated hatred in their menacing eyes. The three demons that were in front of the gate moved on the side, and the gate opened up on its own accord. I walked through the gate. It was very hot and I started sweating again. I saw these demons and they were chanting in their own language that I could not understand.

As I continued through the gate, I saw worms on both sides of the gates and the stench of rotting flesh filled the air. Suddenly I heard again a loud sound like metals grinding against each other, and I started sweating again. As I continued through the gate of hell, I also heard loud noises again like "Dang, dang, dang, dong, dong, dong" and then I heard laughter that sounded like "Ha, ha, ha." Suddenly I heard what sounded like thousands upon thousands of screams, and when I looked around, I saw an innumerable amount of souls screaming and crying. The demons continuously tortured these souls with what appeared to be pitchforks that were about six feet long. As I continued through the gate, many of the souls that saw me cried, "Help me please, help me please." Worms were eating their flesh. My heart became filled with great sorrow and I started to cry again because of the torment and the agony that these souls were experiencing. I realized that there was no hope or redemption for these souls for they were damned, and even throughout all of this, the demons seemed to sadistically enjoy inflicting pain on these souls, and they laughed as they did it.

I want to interject and say to my readers again that hell is the destination of people who do not accept Jesus Christ as there Lord and Savior or serve him while they were here on earth, and Jesus says in hell, the worms do not die and the fire is not quenched. The Bible says in Isaiah 5:14, "Therefore hell hath enlarged herself, and opened her mouth without measure: and their glory, and their multitude, and their pomp, and he that rejoiceth, shall descend into it."

As I journeyed through the gate of hell, suddenly I saw again a demon on the second stage of the gate, and he was very tall and he had one eye in the middle of his forehead. He had in his hand a chain that was about seven feet long and it had a ball with spikes on its end. As I looked forward, I saw many hooded demons on this long large rock and suddenly the demons started chanting in this language that I could not understand. They had different colored hoods, but I could not see their faces; I could see only their hands. As I continued on, I saw again molten fire everywhere. I also heard the deafening sounds of the screams and cries of millions of men and souls, and they were saying, "Oh, Lord, give me another chance please, please stop, please stop." My heart got full again and I began to cry because I heard these men crying and asking for help and I could not help because they were lost forever. I heard the demons laughing "He, he, he, ha, ha, ha." I also heard the reverberating sound "Doom, doom." The sound was everywhere, and I stared but could not discern where the sounds came from.

Suddenly I found myself out of the eleventh gate. As I continued on the road of hell, I again looked in the distance and I saw many hundreds gates that were about nine feet high, and this appeared to be a main checkpoint of hell. As I approached the gate, they opened simultaneously and demons came out of each gate. They all had human heads with animal ears, and their bodies were like gremlin bodies. Their hands—I mean, claws— were half-red and half-black and they smelled terrible. As I reached within ten feet of these demons, they looked at each other, and afterward, they stared menacingly at me, but that was all they could do because I was protected by the Spirit of the Lord. I was not allowed to go through those gates.

Afterward I took a right turn and suddenly I came to this huge gate, and the Lord said to me, "This is the twelfth gate." The gate had a huge rusty lock on it, and suddenly the gate opened on its own accord. I went in and saw molten fire everywhere, and the stench of rotting flesh filled the air. As I passed through I heard many demons laughing and chanting. As I continued through the gate, I heard again thousands upon thousands of screams, and when I looked around, I saw an innumerable amount of souls screaming and crying. Demons were laughing and dancing, and they were torturing these souls with what appeared to be pitchforks. As I continued on, I saw that many of the souls started grabbing and pulling each other, and the souls that saw me cried and said, "Help me, help me." Worms continued to engulf their flesh. I realized that there was no hope or redemption for these souls for they were eternally damned.

As I continued through the gate, I saw these two demons who had two heads and one eye and were about seven feet tall, and each one of them had human heads and the next head was in human form. They had long tails and their feet were curled up. On top of their heads were six horns, and their faces were full of marks. They had four sharp teeth coming out of their mouths. They had long spears in their hands. They looked at me and I could see the deep-seated hatred in their menacing eyes. Worms were oozing from their bodies. As I continued on, I heard again long sounds like "Ching, ching, ching" and then laughter, "Ha, ha, ha, ching, ching, chin."

I would like to mention at this time that the sound that I heard in hell I am trying to describe to the best of my ability. I have never heard any of the sounds on earth such as these sounds. I stood amazed at what I was hearing as I walk through these gates and tunnels.

As I continued on, I saw four demonic angels with four wings, and they were about eight feet tall. Two of them had heads like that of snakes and the other two had heads shaped like that of dragons. They were full of scales and they had thick chains in their hands, and each one of them had three horns on their heads, and their eyes were red. I was astonished at what I saw. As I proceeded, I saw again molten fire everywhere and I heard again many screams. As I continued, the gate suddenly opened wide, and I saw literally thousands of people souls, and they were crying, reaching, and saying, "Help me, help me, take me from this place." They were surrounded by demons who had pitchforks in their hands.

As I continued through the gate of hell, suddenly I saw three chairs made of stone, and sitting on these chairs were three huge demons that had goat horns on top of their heads. Imps were around them and they were dressed completely in red, and they were hideous, disfigured, and thick. They had what appeared to be long swords in their hands, and the imps started to chat in their own language. I perceived that these demons on these chairs had position and power in the kingdom of darkness. Their eyes were green and they stared menacingly at me for what appeared to be fifth teen minutes, and I was astonished and dumbfounded at what I had seen for what appeared to be about ten minutes. When I came to myself or senses, I heard multitudes of people crying and screaming, but I did not see them.

At this time I again began to sweat profusely. I was frightened, nervous, and amazed at what I was experiencing, and even though the Holy Spirit was with me, I was still allowed to experience the overwhelming terror and helplessness of the eternally damned. As I continued through the gate, I saw three hooded demons with their backs to me, and they turned around. I saw that they had spears in their hands, and they stared at me for what appeared to be about ten minutes, and I said to myself, "What are their intentions?" They started laughing, "Ha, ha, ha, haha, hehehe." They were about eight feet tall and they smelled stinky.

As I continued on, I heard a voice of a man, and he was saying, "I did not mean to make love with that woman's husband." I continued to follow the voice until I saw this man, and his body was infested with worms, and when he saw me he said, "Please, please give me some water for I am thirsty bad. Tell my family and friends don't come here. Take me from this place." After witnessing the state of this man, I became terrified. I realized that there was no hope or redemption for this man.

Suddenly I found myself out of the twelfth gate. I woke up out of the vision.

For many people that do not believe that hell is real, I come to you to let you know that I am a living witness the Spirit of the Living God, who took me there. Please don't play around with your one soul. The Spirit of the Living God said to me, "Let them know that hell is real." If you look at what is happening in the world, we can surely see the imminent return of our Lord our God, so let us prepare to meet our God. Satan does not love you. All he wants is to destroy your soul. If you have not given your heart to the Lord, this is a wonderful time to do it. Just say this prayer: Heavenly Father, in the name of your Son, Jesus, I ask you to come into my life, to be my Lord and Savior. I ask that you cleanse me from every sin, for I believe that Jesus Christ died on Calvary's cross for my sins, and I believe that he arose from the dead and is seated on the right-hand side of the Father and is making intercessions for me right now. Thank you, Jesus, for coming into my heart and being my Lord and Savior. I promise to serve you all my days. Amen.

Apostle Wislet Charles

2426982420;2424238827
wisletcharles@gmail.com

GARDEN HILLS #2
FRANGIPANI AVENUE
P.O. BOX SB 50436
NASSAU, BAHAMAS

www.ingramcontent.com/pod-product-compliance
Lightning Source LLC
Chambersburg PA
CBHW061808050726

47598CB00002B/918